W9-CFK-004

Would You Rather?

Family Challenge!

EDITION

Would You Rather?

Family Challenge!

EDITION

Hilarious Scenarios
& Crazy Competition
for Kids, Teens, and Adults

LINDSEY DALY

Z KIDS · NEW YORK

Copyright © 2021 by Penguin Random House LLC

All rights reserved.

Published in the United States by Z Kids, an imprint of
Zeitgeist™, a division of Random House LLC, New York.

penguinrandomhouse.com

Zeitgeist™ is a trademark of Penguin Random House LLC

ISBN: 9780593435465
Ebook ISBN: 9780593435472
Proprietary ISBN: 9780525615460

Cover art © Shutterstock.com/Andrii Symonenko
Interior art © Shutterstock.com/mhatzapa
Author photograph by Jocelyn Morales
Book design by Katy Brown

Printed in the United States of America

1 3 5 7 9 10 8 6 4 2

For Mom, Dad, and Andrew, always
&
Mike, Liz, Nicole, Meghan, and Kayla,
my friends who feel like family

Contents

Introduction

My first book, *Would You Rather? Made You Think! Edition*, showed you a fun way to express your creativity in the classroom and with your families. Whether it was in person or over Zoom, you demonstrated just how smart and funny you truly are. You had hilarious, thought-provoking conversations and learned more about your peers through laughter and dialogue. You didn't think I'd stop there, did you? *Would You Rather? Family Challenge! Edition* keeps the critical-thinking party going with over 160 new humorous and interesting scenarios for your whole family to enjoy.

So, let's refresh our memory: What is "critical thinking"? In simple terms, it is considering all of the possibilities around any given topic and forming your own opinion. Much like a toddler who just started talking, thinking critically means learning information and immediately asking, "Why?"

The world NEEDS critical thinkers! Without those skills, Albert Einstein would have never developed the theory of relativity. Martin Luther King, Jr. wouldn't have led the civil rights movement. Malala Yousafzai would have never become an education activist. What do they all have in common? They questioned. They brainstormed. They didn't give up until their thoughts changed the world. They did ALL of their chores without ever being asked! Okay, I can't confirm the last one, but I'm just trying to help your parents out. If these critical thinkers could use their brain power to chase their dreams, so can you!

Start the habit of critical thinking now. Whether you're book smart, street smart, art smart, or all three, this is your time to shine!

Rules of the Game

FOR THREE PLAYERS OR MORE:

* Get a group of friends or family members together for a game of wits and creativity. The more the merrier!
* The game is played in 8 rounds with 20 questions in each round.
* Players rotate the responsibility of being the "judge" and read the question aloud to the group.
* Players will have one minute to develop their answer with an explanation. Players will take turns sharing their answers.
* The judge of that round will then select the answer they enjoyed the most based on humor, creativity, or logic. The player whose answer was chosen will be awarded the point for that question.

* When players complete the round, points will be tallied and someone will be named the winner for that round.
* When players complete the entire book, points will be tallied again to determine the champion.
* In the event of a tie, see the "tie breaker" question at the end of each round. This should only be used for the two players who are tied. All of the remaining players will vote on the best answer.

FOR TWO PLAYERS:

* If you promise to be fair, you can follow the same rules used for three or more players, with both players taking turns at being the judge.
* If not, then each player is given 5 points to award per question. Both players must assign the 5 points in 3 categories: logic, humor, and creativity. Add up the points at the end of each round to see who wins that round!

ROUND

1

Super Science

Would you rather

spend a year working in a top-secret science lab

or

on the International Space Station?

WINNER: POINTS:

Would you rather

dissect a scorpion

or

a tarantula?

WINNER: POINTS:

Would you rather

invent a spaceship that could travel to Mars

or

a device that rids the air of pollutants?

WINNER: POINTS:

Would you rather

discover the bones of the world's first human

or

the world's oldest living reptile?

WINNER: POINTS:

Would you rather
create an app that locates
missing pets
or
predicts the winning
lottery numbers?

WINNER: POINTS:

Would you rather
chase a tornado in a car
or
stand on top of a skyscraper
during a lightning storm?

WINNER: POINTS:

Would you rather
spend a year studying
volcanic ash
or
the Earth's crust?

WINNER: POINTS:

Would you rather
watch a solar eclipse
or
a meteor shower?

WINNER: POINTS:

Would you rather
have a planetarium
in your home
or
a greenhouse full of
exotic plants?

WINNER: POINTS:

Would you rather
develop a vaccine that prevents
people from itching
or
stops people from feeling cold?

WINNER: POINTS:

Would you rather

be fluent in writing HTML code

or

know how to hack your favorite
video game so you always win?

WINNER: POINTS:

Would you rather

spend an hour
floating around in space

or

swimming in the depths
of the ocean?

WINNER: POINTS:

Would you rather
have an arm made of gold
or
aluminum?

WINNER: POINTS:

Would you rather
examine parasites
under a microscope
or
a new strain of bacteria?

WINNER: POINTS:

WOULD YOU RATHER?

Would you rather
discover a new element
or
a new mineral?

WINNER: POINTS:

Would you rather
save Earth from plummeting
into a black hole
or
being hit by a large meteor?

WINNER: POINTS:

Would you rather
discover a faster method of air travel
or
land travel?

WINNER: POINTS:

Would you rather
research plants in the
Amazon rain forest
or
rock formations in the
Grand Canyon?

WINNER: POINTS:

Would you rather
own a star
or
a piece of coral from the
Great Barrier Reef?

WINNER: POINTS:

Would you rather
accidentally set a science lab on fire
during an experiment
or
get a dangerous chemical
in your eye?

WINNER: POINTS:

Would you rather

watch how fireworks are made

or

jet packs?

WINNER: POINTS:

WINNER

ROUND 1

WINNER:
_____

TOTAL POINTS:
_____

ROUND

2

Nifty Nature

Would you rather
have a pet owl
or
giraffe?

WINNER: POINTS:

Would you rather
watch baby birds hatching
or
baby sea turtles?

WINNER: POINTS:

WOULD YOU RATHER?

Would you rather
get thrown up on by your dog
or
licked by your cat after it
just cleaned itself?

WINNER: POINTS:

Would you rather
play on a rope swing over a creek
or
go white water rafting down a river?

WINNER: POINTS:

Would you rather
raise a baby bunny that has been
separated from its mother
or
nurse a bird with a hurt
wing back to health?

WINNER: POINTS:

Would you rather
walk through a spider web
or
a pricker bush?

WINNER: POINTS:

Would you rather
play hide-and-seek
in a dense forest
or
a cornfield with cornstalks
taller than your head?

WINNER: POINTS:

Would you rather
get knocked over by a giant wave
or
caught outside in a hail storm?

WINNER: POINTS:

Would you rather
eat a live toad
or
a dead rattlesnake?

WINNER: POINTS:

Would you rather
fall face-first into a
hornet's nest
or
a pile of horse manure?

WINNER: POINTS:

Would you rather

hike ten miles in the pouring rain

or

bike five miles in the sweltering heat?

WINNER: POINTS:

Would you rather

use wet leaves as toilet paper

or

tree bark?

WINNER: POINTS:

Would you rather
spend a night in
an igloo wearing only
your bathing suit
or
the middle of a forest
during a thunderstorm?

WINNER: POINTS:

Would you rather
give a piggyback ride to a penguin
or
a sloth?

WINNER: POINTS:

Would you rather
build a shelter using cacti
or
bamboo sticks?

WINNER: POINTS:

Would you rather
prevent wildfires
or
eliminate all of the trash in
the world's oceans?

WINNER: POINTS:

Would you rather
be caught in a volcanic eruption
or
an avalanche?

WINNER: POINTS:

Would you rather
spend the day playing in an
overgrown meadow
or
a tree house?

WINNER: POINTS:

Would you rather
wake up covered in centipedes
or
worms?

WINNER: POINTS:

Would you rather
be a stink bug for a week
or
a cockroach?

WINNER: POINTS:

Would you rather
hug a jellyfish
or
a stingray?

WINNER: POINTS:

WINNER

WINNER:
_____

TOTAL POINTS:
_____

ROUND

3

Serious Sports

Would you rather
get hit with a foul ball
at a baseball game
or
tackled by a football player?

WINNER: POINTS:

Would you rather
play your personal best but your
team loses
or
play the worst game of your
life but your team wins?

WINNER: POINTS:

Would you rather

compete in a swimming race
wearing a gorilla costume

or

a hazmat suit?

WINNER: POINTS:

Would you rather

ride in the passenger seat
of a car in a NASCAR race

or

on the back of a horse in
the Kentucky Derby?

WINNER: POINTS:

Would you rather
be the caddy for a professional golfer
or
the ball person during
a tennis match?

WINNER: POINTS:

Would you rather
win front-row tickets
to the Super Bowl
or
play a one-on-one game against
your favorite athlete?

WINNER: POINTS:

Would you rather
be thrown into a skateboarding
competition without any experience
or
a surfing competition?

WINNER: POINTS:

Would you rather
be a professional polo player
or
bowler?

WINNER: POINTS:

Would you rather
race someone on a Jet Ski
or
a dirt bike?

WINNER: POINTS:

Would you rather
wrestle someone 50 pounds
heavier than you
or
face professional players
in a rugby match?

WINNER: POINTS:

Would you rather
make the game-winning
basket at the buzzer
or
hit a home run in the final inning?

WINNER: POINTS:

Would you rather
be the best player on a horrible team
or
the worst player on the best team?

WINNER: POINTS:

Would you rather
compete in an archery tournament
or
a bobsled race?

WINNER: POINTS:

Would you rather
be chosen team captain over
your best friend
or
have your best friend be
picked instead of you?

WINNER: POINTS:

Would you rather
your team lose a championship
game by 1 point
or
50 points?

WINNER: POINTS:

Would you rather
have an ice-skating rink
in your backyard
or
an Olympic-size swimming pool?

WINNER: POINTS:

Would you rather
be a referee for professional sporting events
or
a commentator?

WINNER: POINTS:

Would you rather
play beach volleyball when it's snowing
or
100 degrees?

WINNER: POINTS:

Would you rather
be a flyer at the top of a
cheerleading pyramid
or
on a synchronized
ice-skating team?

WINNER: POINTS:

Would you rather
be a competitive dancer
or
an acrobat in a traveling circus?

WINNER: POINTS:

Would you rather

run a marathon in snow boots

or

fancy dress shoes?

WINNER: POINTS:

WINNER:
_____

TOTAL POINTS:
_____

ROUND

4

Hilarious History

Would you rather
discover the diary
of a Roman emperor
or
a Founding Father
of the United States?

WINNER: POINTS:

Would you rather
have been in the audience
for Martin Luther King, Jr.'s
"I Have a Dream" speech
or
Abraham Lincoln's
"Gettysburg Address"?

WINNER: POINTS:

Would you rather
have a one-on-one lesson
with Socrates
or
Albert Einstein?

WINNER: POINTS:

Would you rather
be able to go back in time and
change one historical event
or
see 200 years into the future but
not be able to change anything?

WINNER: POINTS:

Would you rather
fall down the stairs
of the Lincoln Memorial
or
get stuck in the elevator inside
the Washington Monument?

WINNER: POINTS:

Would you rather
be a member of the CIA
or
the Secret Service?

WINNER: POINTS:

Would you rather
accidentally break an ancient
vase in a museum
or
damage the original US
Constitution by touching it?

WINNER: POINTS:

Would you rather
have a sleepover with friends
in a famous museum
or
the White House?

WINNER: POINTS:

Would you rather
find out that you're a descendant
of a former US president
or
a medieval king?

WINNER: POINTS:

Would you rather
interview a military general
or
an FBI agent?

WINNER: POINTS:

Would you rather
be a history teacher
or
a museum tour guide?

WINNER: POINTS:

Would you rather
play *Fortnite* against
the queen of England
or
Among Us against
the prime minister of Canada?

WINNER: POINTS:

Would you rather
be a presidential speechwriter
or
a member of Congress?

WINNER: POINTS:

Would you rather
hold a medieval sword
or
try on an ancient Egyptian
headdress?

WINNER: POINTS:

WOULD YOU RATHER?

Would you rather
be a court jester
during the Middle Ages
or
the king's food taster?

WINNER: POINTS:

Would you rather
be awarded the Nobel Peace Prize
or
the Presidential Medal of Freedom?

WINNER: POINTS:

Would you rather
be a Supreme Court justice
or
a United Nations ambassador?

WINNER: POINTS:

Would you rather
be a cowboy or cowgirl
in the Wild West
or
a jazz musician during the
Roaring Twenties?

WINNER: POINTS:

Would you rather

spend the night alone
on a former battlefield

or

in Arlington National Cemetery?

WINNER: POINTS:

Would you rather

accidentally sneeze in the
face of a famous activist

or

the president of the United States?

WINNER: POINTS:

Would you rather

help repair the Great Wall of China

or

the Great Pyramids?

WINNER: POINTS:

WINNER

ROUND

4

WINNER:
_____

TOTAL POINTS:
_____

5

Essential
Entertainment

Would you rather
be the star of a Broadway show
that nobody liked
or
the author of a book that
got bad reviews?

WINNER: POINTS:

Would you rather
spend a day shadowing an animator
or
a CGI (computer-
generated images) artist?

WINNER: POINTS:

Would you rather
be pranked by a
famous YouTube star
or
surprised by your favorite celebrity?

WINNER: POINTS:

Would you rather
be an extra in a film
or
a stunt double?

WINNER: POINTS:

Would you rather
take a six-hour mime class
or
perform magic tricks at a five-year-old's birthday party?

WINNER: POINTS:

Would you rather
be a talented actor that
few have heard of
or
an average actor known by all?

WINNER: POINTS:

Would you rather
be a backup dancer
for a famous singer
or
a news reporter?

WINNER: POINTS:

Would you rather
star in a reality television show
that documents your life
or
be the host of a popular podcast?

WINNER: POINTS:

Would you rather
try stand-up comedy
and completely bomb
or
have your voice crack while
singing for an audience?

WINNER: POINTS:

Would you rather
represent celebrities
as their publicist
or
lawyer?

WINNER: POINTS:

Would you rather

be prevented from
watching your favorite
movie again

or

listening to your favorite song?

WINNER: POINTS:

Would you rather

get a private tour of the set of your
favorite television show

or

have a five-minute conversation
with your favorite actor?

WINNER: POINTS:

Would you rather
learn how to perform stage combat
or
make elaborate costumes?

WINNER: POINTS:

Would you rather
do a dramatic poetry reading in front
of your neighbors
or
perform a tap-dancing routine?

WINNER: POINTS:

Would you rather
tour the world as a member
of a ten-person band
or
a solo artist?

WINNER: POINTS:

Would you rather
host an awards show
or
interview celebrities on
the red carpet?

WINNER: POINTS:

Would you rather
get paid to play video games
or
review books?

WINNER: POINTS:

Would you rather
entertain children at an
amusement park dressed
as an animal
or
a clown?

WINNER: POINTS:

Would you rather

go crowd-surfing during a concert

or

dance onstage?

WINNER: POINTS:

Would you rather

be a contestant on a game show that
tests your mental abilities

or

your physical strength?

WINNER: POINTS:

Would you rather

attend a concert where the only instrument played is an accordion

or

a tambourine?

WINNER: POINTS:

WINNER:
_____

TOTAL POINTS:
_____

6

Genius
Geography

Would you rather
spend a summer traveling
to every city in Europe
or
Asia?

WINNER: POINTS:

Would you rather
draw maps for a living
or
be an archaeologist?

WINNER: POINTS:

Would you rather
hike every mountain
in North America
or
kayak across all of the Great Lakes?

WINNER: POINTS:

Would you rather
live in an isolated cabin for a year
or
the world's most crowded city?

WINNER: POINTS:

Would you rather
own an island
or
a private lake?

WINNER: POINTS:

Would you rather
spend a month living in
a tent in Antarctica
or
the Sahara Desert?

WINNER: POINTS:

Would you rather
sail across the Atlantic Ocean
or
walk the entire length of California?

WINNER: POINTS:

Would you rather
go zip-lining over the Arenal
Volcano in Costa Rica
or
skydiving in Sydney, Australia?

WINNER: POINTS:

Would you rather
go snow tubing down Mt. Everest
or
roller-skating on the
Great Wall of China?

WINNER: POINTS:

Would you rather
go snorkeling in the
Great Barrier Reef
or
rock climbing at Yosemite
National Park?

WINNER: POINTS:

Would you rather
closely examine a glacier
or
lava on a dormant volcano?

WINNER: POINTS:

Would you rather
take aerial pictures of rivers
or
photograph underground caverns?

WINNER: POINTS:

Would you rather
spend one day in every
country in the world
or
visit 20 countries but spend as much
time as you wanted exploring them?

WINNER: POINTS:

Would you rather
climb to the top of
the Eiffel Tower
or
Machu Picchu?

WINNER: POINTS:

Would you rather
go surfing down a huge sand dune
or
relax in a hot spring?

WINNER: POINTS:

Would you rather
go on an African safari
or
visit an elephant sanctuary
in Thailand?

WINNER: POINTS:

Would you rather
tour Brazil by helicopter
or
London from the top of a
double-decker bus?

WINNER: POINTS:

Would you rather
study the effects
of hurricanes
or
droughts?

WINNER: POINTS:

Would you rather

discover a way to prevent glaciers
from melting

or

earthquakes from happening?

WINNER: POINTS:

Would you rather

watch the sunrise from
a beach in Hawaii

or

the sunset from the top
of Mount Fuji?

WINNER: POINTS:

Would you rather
find your way through a vast forest
using only a compass
or
a poorly drawn map?

WINNER: POINTS:

WINNER: _____

TOTAL POINTS: _____

ROUND

7

Astonishing Arts

Would you rather
be given the *Mona Lisa*
by Leonardo da Vinci
or
Starry Night by Vincent van Gogh?

WINNER: POINTS:

Would you rather
jump into a pool filled with paint
or
a huge pile of glitter?

WINNER: POINTS:

Would you rather
watch Shakespeare perform
one of his plays
or
listen to Mozart play piano?

WINNER: POINTS:

Would you rather
work in an art gallery
or
be an art therapist for kids?

WINNER: POINTS:

Would you rather
compose a symphony
or
choreograph a ballet?

WINNER: POINTS:

Would you rather
take a class on graffiti painting
or
glassblowing?

WINNER: POINTS:

Would you rather
learn how to play
the violin
or
the tuba?

WINNER: POINTS:

Would you rather
dance in a flash mob
or
sing with an a cappella group?

WINNER: POINTS:

Would you rather
sit perfectly still for two hours to
pose for a sculpture class
or
run and jump constantly for
an exercise photo shoot?

WINNER: POINTS:

Would you rather
be a makeup artist
for a horror film
or
a set designer?

WINNER: POINTS:

Would you rather
be a jeweler
or
make wax figures?

WINNER: POINTS:

Would you rather
create art out of recycled materials
or
food products?

WINNER: POINTS:

Would you rather
be a famous fashion
designer of baby clothing
or
pet accessories?

WINNER: POINTS:

Would you rather
take a private dance lesson with
Misty Copeland
or
a writing workshop with
Suzanne Collins?

WINNER: POINTS:

Would you rather
have one of your designs featured
during New York Fashion Week
or
one of your paintings
shown in a museum?

WINNER: POINTS:

Would you rather
teach a group of senior citizens
how to do a TikTok dance
or
beatbox?

WINNER: POINTS:

Would you rather
learn the art of printmaking
or
calligraphy?

WINNER: POINTS:

Would you rather
be an interior designer
or
a film director?

WINNER: POINTS:

Would you rather
have your face covered
in papier-mâché
or
acrylic paint?

WINNER: POINTS:

Would you rather
be a tattoo artist
or
an illustrator for children's books?

WINNER: POINTS:

Would you rather
have the ability to see a color
that no one else can see
or
hear a musical note that
no one else can hear?

WINNER: POINTS:

WINNER

ROUND 7

WINNER:
_____

TOTAL POINTS:
_____

Fabulous Fantasy

Would you rather
anger Poseidon
or
Zeus?

WINNER: POINTS:

Would you rather
discover a forest where candy
grows on trees
or
live in a house where the
furniture is edible?

WINNER: POINTS:

Would you rather
have a conversation with an alien
or
a robot that can no longer
be controlled by the
humans who created it?

WINNER: POINTS:

Would you rather
be able to change your voice to
mimic whoever you want
or
run twice as fast as the
world's fastest person?

WINNER: POINTS:

Would you rather
find the lost city of Atlantis
or
the Fountain of Youth?

WINNER: POINTS:

Would you rather
be able to charge your electronic
devices with the snap of your fingers
or
generate Wi-Fi by
clapping your hands?

WINNER: POINTS:

Would you rather
have the opportunity to
feed a live dinosaur
or
ride on a woolly
mammoth?

WINNER: POINTS:

Would you rather
have chocolate syrup come out of
your eyes when you cry
or
soda?

WINNER: POINTS:

Would you rather

be abducted by a friendly group of aliens for a week

or

travel back in time to spend a week with cave people?

WINNER: POINTS:

Would you rather

summon a ghost with a Ouija board

or

meet a leprechaun?

WINNER: POINTS:

Would you rather

have a genie grant you three wishes
immediately

or

five wishes over the
span of five years?

WINNER: POINTS:

Would you rather

have a pet that can understand and
speak your language for one full day

or

be able to speak to wild animals
whenever you want?

WINNER: POINTS:

Would you rather

get stuck in an alternate
universe where people sing
to express their feelings
or
people are incapable of lying?

WINNER: POINTS:

Would you rather

drink a magic potion that gives you
the ability to walk through walls
or
pause time?

WINNER: POINTS:

Would you rather
have confetti fly out of your nose
every time you sneeze
or
sugar?

WINNER: POINTS:

Would you rather
have the ability to breathe
underwater
or
be invisible for one day each month?

WINNER: POINTS:

Would you rather
never need to sleep
or
use the bathroom?

WINNER: POINTS:

Would you rather
have a fire-breathing dragon
as a pet
or
a werewolf?

WINNER: POINTS:

Would you rather
be taken captive by
a group of
garden gnomes
or
fairies?

WINNER: POINTS:

Would you rather
wake up on a train with no conductor
or
a bus driven by a zombie?

WINNER: POINTS:

Would you rather

walk through a secret door that takes you back in time to a medieval European town

or

a colonial American city?

WINNER: POINTS:

WINNER

ROUND 8

WINNER:
_____

TOTAL POINTS:
_____

WINNER

Would You
Rather?

FAMILY CHALLENGE!
EDITION

This certificate
is awarded to

_____

for being ferociously funny,
captivatingly creative, super smart,
and the winner of wit.

A person who can explain AND
entertain!

CONGRATULATIONS!

About the Author

 Lindsey Daly grew up in Andover, New Jersey. She graduated from Ramapo College of New Jersey with a BA in history and a certification in secondary education. Lindsey is a middle school social studies teacher and the author of *Would You Rather? Made You Think! Edition*. She lives with her dog, Teddy, in New Jersey.

Instagram: **@lindseydalybooks**

Twitter: **@LindseyDaly10**